AF228568

Law Enforcement

PATROL COPS

John Hamilton

ABDOBOOKS.COM

Published by Abdo Publishing, a division of ABDO, PO Box 398166, Minneapolis, Minnesota 55439. Copyright © 2021 by Abdo Consulting Group, Inc. International copyrights reserved in all countries. No part of this book may be reproduced in any form without written permission from the publisher. Abdo & Daughters™ is a trademark and logo of Abdo Publishing.

Printed in the United States of America, North Mankato, Minnesota.

022020

092020

Editor: Sue Hamilton

Copy Editor: Bridget O'Brien

Creative Director: Dorothy Toth

Graphic Design: John Hamilton

Cover Design: Victoria Bates

Cover Photo: iStock

Interior Images: Alamy-pgs 17, 27, 43; AP-pgs 15, 18, 19, 24, 25; Axon Enterprise, Inc.-pg 31; Gilbert Police Department-pg 16; iStock-pgs 1, 4, 5, 6, 9, 10, 11, 12, 21, 22, 23, 28, 29, 30, 37, 39, 45; John Hamilton-pgs 7, 34; Shutterstock-pgs 33, 41, 42.

LIBRARY OF CONGRESS CONTROL NUMBER: 2019956067

PUBLISHER'S CATALOGING-IN-PUBLICATION DATA

Names: Hamilton, John, author.

Title: Patrol cops / by John Hamilton

Description: Minneapolis, Minnesota : Abdo Publishing, 2021 | Series: Law enforcement | Includes online resources and index

Identifiers: ISBN 9781532193873 (lib. bdg.) | ISBN 9781098212650 (ebook)

Subjects: LCSH: Law enforcement--Juvenile literature. | Police patrol--Juvenile literature. | Officers--Juvenile literature.

Classification: DDC 363.2--dc23

TABLE OF CONTENTS

Chapter 1

COPS ON PATROL

Almost all police officers begin their careers as patrol cops. Whether they later become detectives, SWAT team members, or even department chiefs, cops start out by patrolling the streets. They stop crime and protect lives and property. It is the biggest reason why most cops choose a law enforcement career.

Police work isn't just about catching bad guys. The job also requires a lot of paperwork and meetings. Stress can also take a toll on a cop's mental health. Despite the hardships and dangers, many officers spend their entire careers as patrol cops. It is a fulfilling job. Every day, police officers can make a difference in people's lives.

Patrol officers do many things, but their main job is to stop crime and protect lives and property.

Most police officers patrol the streets in squad cars, which are fast, carry equipment, and can be used as shields.

Patrol cops make arrests when suspects break laws. They also respond when people are in danger and need help.

Many patrol officers work for cities. Others work for county sheriff's departments or become state troopers. No matter what agency they work for, patrol cops are highly trained. They usually must attend and pass a monthslong police academy before they can even start patrolling the streets. Once they become fully qualified, they must continue their education and training throughout their careers.

When people think of cops, they usually think of patrol officers. They are the ones who wear the department uniform and badges of their city, county, or state. They are the first line of defense against lawbreakers. Whether they are enforcing traffic laws, responding to accidents, or catching wanted criminals, patrol cops are almost always the first on the scene when help is needed.

Community policing

A very important way that patrol cops can be more effective is to be a part of the communities they serve. In addition to building goodwill, police officers use their ties with citizens to solve crimes and help with other issues that affect people. This is called community policing.

Police officers make connections by building partnerships with groups such as local businesses, churches, and schools. These partnerships make communities better places in which to live and work.

McGruff the Crime Dog at a community gathering.

Chapter 2

AN AVERAGE DAY

For patrol cops, every shift has its own ups and downs. The job has many challenges. The pay and benefits are good, but police officers often deal with hardships and tragedies. However, the satisfaction of helping people is so great that many cops stay on the force for years, often for a lifetime.

Cops work in shifts, either during the day or at night. (Night shift is nicknamed the graveyard shift, or dogwatch.) Before a shift begins, officers gather at the police station for roll call. It lasts about 30 minutes. After inspection, a shift sergeant gives out any special assignments. The sergeant also informs officers of any BOLO (be-on-the-lookout) alerts.

In service

After dismissal, officers grab a cup of coffee or bottle of water, and then inspect their squad cars and equipment, including weapons, first aid kits, and radar units. When everything is in order, they radio the police dispatcher that they are "10-8" (in service). Then they drive out of the police lot and onto the city streets to begin their patrols.

For patrol officers, there is no such thing as an "average" day. Each shift is unique, with its own challenges.

On patrol

When cruising the streets, cops are either on patrol or on service calls. When they are on patrol, they are actively looking for lawbreakers or citizens in trouble. They may slowly drive past businesses and homes late at night, on alert for suspicious activity. If a door or window appears to have been broken into, officers will investigate for a possible burglary or other crimes.

If cops come upon a crime in progress, such as a fight or obvious drug deal, they may immediately make arrests. If they are the first on the scene of an auto accident, they are trained to give medical assistance until paramedics arrive.

Protecting the community

Much of the time spent on patrol includes traffic duty. Cops are always on the lookout for drivers who are speeding, weaving out of their lanes, or ignoring stop signs. It is a patrol officer's duty to protect law-abiding citizens from such dangerous behavior.

Some people think cops are bullies who are hated by their communities, but that is far from the truth. Even in the most crime-ridden parts of a city, police officers are welcomed by the majority of citizens who live there. Strangers often approach cops to thank them for patrolling their neighborhoods.

During a traffic emergency, such as a crash, patrol officers are often the first ones on the scene to give assistance.

Calls for service

When cops aren't patrolling the streets, they stay busy answering calls for service. These are requests received from dispatchers at police headquarters, usually using the 911 emergency phone system. Service calls often involve solving problems that people have, such as domestic violence or other kinds of trouble within families. Other common examples include traffic accidents, trespassing, and disorderly conduct.

Many 911 calls are not true emergencies, but cops treat all service calls with urgency. It is common for several officers to arrive at the scene to back each other up, even if a call turns out to be minor. Some people fake emergencies to trick police into responding faster. This can result in dangerous situations. Officers might race to a caller's address, guns drawn, without any real information of what they'll find at the scene. Most calls for service, however, are real. Citizens in trouble are always happy to see the flashing lights of approaching police vehicles.

WHAT DOES COP MEAN?

Many people believe the word "cop" is short for "constable on patrol," or that it refers to the shiny copper buttons worn by British policemen of the early 1800s. Neither is accurate. In the English language, the verb "cop" means "to catch or seize." In the mid-1800s, people who were arrested by the police were said to be "copped." Policemen were then called "coppers," which is shortened today as "cops."

Chapter 3

BECOMING A POLICE OFFICER

Law enforcement is a very demanding career, but it is also exciting and rewarding. Men and women from many different backgrounds want to become cops. Getting hired is a long process, and competition is high.

Each state has its own requirements for becoming a sworn police officer. Applicants must be at least 21 years old. A degree in criminal justice is sometimes an advantage. Military experience is also a plus.

Tests and screenings

The first step in the process is to fill out a written application (usually online) for a city or agency that is hiring. When completed, the department will do a screening to make sure applicants are not convicted felons.

If applicants are chosen, they take a written exam. It tests skills such as decision-making, memory, and ethics. Candidates then take a physical agility test. It measures strength, endurance, and general fitness. Tests vary from state to state, but most include push-ups, sit-ups, and a timed run.

New Jersey State Police recruits run as part of a physical qualification test at a training academy.

If candidates pass the written exam and agility test, the next step is to answer questions in front of a small group of examiners. This "oral board" is made up of experienced, high-ranking police officers. The exam takes about 30 minutes.

Good cops need to remain calm at all times, yet behave with confidence and authority. Oral board questions are designed to test how candidates might react in difficult, real-world situations. One example: "You respond to a call for help and arrive at a private home. A person can be heard screaming upstairs. A group of armed men at the front entrance prevents you from entering. You radio for help, but are told backup won't arrive for 30 minutes. The screaming inside the house continues. What do you do?" In many cases, there is no "right" or "wrong" answer. The examiners want to see how candidates might react under pressure.

A candidate answers questions during her oral board exam at the Gilbert, AZ, police department.

After the oral exam, candidates take a polygraph (or lie detector) test about their personal history, plus a psychological exam. A background investigation is also conducted by police detectives to make sure candidates have been truthful.

If all goes well, candidates receive a letter offering them employment as a police officer. The next step is to pass a final medical exam and a drug test. After that, in most states candidates are told to report for training at a police academy.

THE POLICE ACADEMY

The police academy is the first phase of training for law enforcement officers. In many ways, it is like attending a military boot camp. Training is rigorous and physically challenging. The main goal is to prepare for the hazards of the job. Knowledge and discipline can mean the difference between life and death in the real world.

Large cities often run their own police academies. Smaller cities or agencies may pool their resources and share an academy with recruits from several different police forces. Recruits usually live at the academy while they learn. Training can take from five to eight months, depending on state requirements.

A Pennsylvania State Police instructor teaches a class at the State Police Academy in Hershey, PA.

Police academy recruits split their time between classroom work and physical training. They learn about local and federal laws, department policies, ethics, and how to process crime reports. Physical training includes learning how to handle firearms and other weapons, hand-to-hand combat, handcuffing, high-speed driver training, physical fitness, and many more skills needed to safely patrol the streets and investigate crimes.

As an instructor monitors their progress, police recruits practice self-defense techniques in Burien, WA.

Chapter 5

ADVANCED TRAINING

After graduating from the police academy, new officers take the next step in their training. This involves riding in a patrol car with a field training officer (FTO). FTOs help new officers apply what they've learned at the police academy to the real world. Officer safety is stressed. FTO evaluations last several months until new officers are ready to patrol the streets on their own.

Learning on the job

Even after getting hired full time, cops continue to take advanced law enforcement classes. This usually continues for the rest of their careers.

Many advanced classes are required, while others are voluntary. For example, cops might be required to receive yearly instruction on how much force is allowed during an arrest. They can also learn about sexual harassment in the workplace, or take other refresher courses. Each state has different requirements for its police officers, but the basics are mostly the same.

When first starting out, rookie cops usually ride with an experienced field training officer.

Using police radar to detect a car's speed is a skill that takes many hours of additional training.

Even though basic skills are taught at police academies, certain specialties require additional classroom lectures and hands-on training. Many common skills that the public sees cops using every day are actually the result of many weeks of learning and testing.

One example is the use of radar speed detectors. Certification requires up to 40 hours of lectures in some states, a written test, and several weeks of training. Then an officer's skills are evaluated. Only after being certified is the officer allowed to use radar to issue tickets for speeding.

Advanced learning

Many police officers want to continue learning in order to increase their skills and climb up the chain of command. Advanced training classes are taught at local police departments or in special training centers. Specific classes aren't required, as long as a minimum number of training hours are completed each year (about 20 to 30 hours).

Common advanced classes include how to handle high-risk situations, such as breaking down doors and entering buildings with people inside shooting at you. Computer classes are becoming very popular. They include techniques for detecting bank fraud or crimes against children.

Other common classes include homicide investigations, search-and-seizure techniques, how to properly use force when making an arrest, SWAT training, canine handling, advanced driving techniques, and firearms qualifications.

An increasing number of police officers are being trained to detect computer files that reveal criminal behavior.

POLICE AGENCIES

Police agencies are groups that enforce the law. They can be local, state, or federal. City police departments are agencies. They hire officers, maintain fleets of patrol vehicles, buy equipment, and work with communities to keep them safe.

Not all cities are big enough to have their own police departments. They rely on other agencies to enforce laws. Sheriff's departments are run by individual counties. These police agencies are led by an elected sheriff. They have a staff of deputies who patrol the counties. In many areas, the sheriff's department is also responsible for running jails and keeping courtrooms safe.

Heavily armed Randall County Sheriff's Department deputies at the scene of a shooting in Amarillo, TX.

Florida Highway Patrol Sergeant Mark Wysocky in front of his patrol cruiser in Sunrise, FL.

State police are responsible for patrolling a state and enforcing its laws. They are often called state troopers, or the highway patrol. They can be seen patrolling highways, but they operate all over a state, even in cities. They also help local and county police agencies with criminal investigations.

Chapter 7

POLICE EQUIPMENT

Patrol officers must have the proper equipment when they respond to crimes. Most equipment is carried on an officer's body at all times. In total, equipment can easily weigh more than 10 pounds (4.5 kg). However, with proper training, these tools of the trade can save an officer's life.

Uniforms

Patrol officers wear distinct uniforms. They vary in style depending on the agency and the season. Uniforms are almost always military-style, with wrinkle-free fabric and sharp creases. Shirts have epaulets on the shoulders. A badge and nameplate are pinned to the front. High-ranking officers, such as sergeants, lieutenants, and captains, wear patches and pins that identify their rank.

Under their shirts, officers wear bullet-resistant vests. These are also called tactical vests, or body armor. They protect the chest and back by keeping most handgun bullets from penetrating the skin. Vests are made of special fabrics such as Kevlar.

A New York City police officer patrolling the streets during a May Day rally in Union Square Park, New York City, NY.

Hard body armor protects against powerful bullets, such as those fired from rifles. The vests have large pockets in which bullet-stopping plates are inserted. The plates are made of a dense, ceramic-like material, or a tough plastic, such as polyethylene. Hard body armor can weigh up to 10 pounds (4.5 kg). It is worn more often by officers with high-risk jobs, such as those on SWAT teams.

Most patrol officers wear soft, bullet-resistant vests. They stop most handgun ammunition from penetrating the skin, but the impact can cause bruising or broken ribs.

Duty belts

Duty belts are thick leather or nylon straps about 2 inches (5 cm) wide. Officers carry several kinds of equipment on their duty belts. This gives them quick access to the tools they need to do their job.

A duty belt holds items that a patrol officer might need quickly, such as a firearm and handcuff keys.

Equipment is usually carried in pouches attached to duty belts. Common items include high-powered flashlights, batons (nightsticks), handcuffs, a radio, keys, pepper spray, spare ammo, and latex gloves. Weapons in holsters are also carried on duty belts.

Firearms

Almost every patrol officer in the United States carries at least one handgun. Modern cops rely on semiautomatic pistols. Most use 9mm, .40-caliber, or .45-caliber ammunition. Semiautomatic pistols fire one round with each pull of the trigger. They normally can fire 8 to 20 rounds of ammunition before needing to be reloaded. Popular pistol brands include Glock, Smith & Wesson, SIG Sauer, Ruger, Heckler and Koch, Colt, and Beretta.

Sometimes patrol cops encounter scenes, such as armed robberies or hostage situations, that require more firepower than a simple handgun. In the past, most patrol cars were equipped with a shotgun, such as the popular Remington 870. Today, many shotguns have been replaced by powerful Colt M4 or AR-15 assault rifles.

Less lethal

Deadly force is not necessary for most situations. Instead of firearms such as pistols and rifles, patrol cops often use weapons that stun or control suspects who flee or become violent. These weapons are called "less lethal." Tragic accidents can happen when these weapons are used. That is why they are not called "non-lethal" weapons. However, they are much less likely to kill when used properly.

Electronic control weapons are less-lethal devices that resemble pistols. They are often called Tasers, after the company that makes many of the models used by law enforcement. Two metal barbs are connected by thin wires to the Taser. The barbs are shot out and stick into the skin, even penetrating through thick clothing. A powerful electrical charge travels through the wires, making a suspect's muscles spasm and stiffen. Suspects can no longer stand or fight. That allows cops to quickly subdue them.

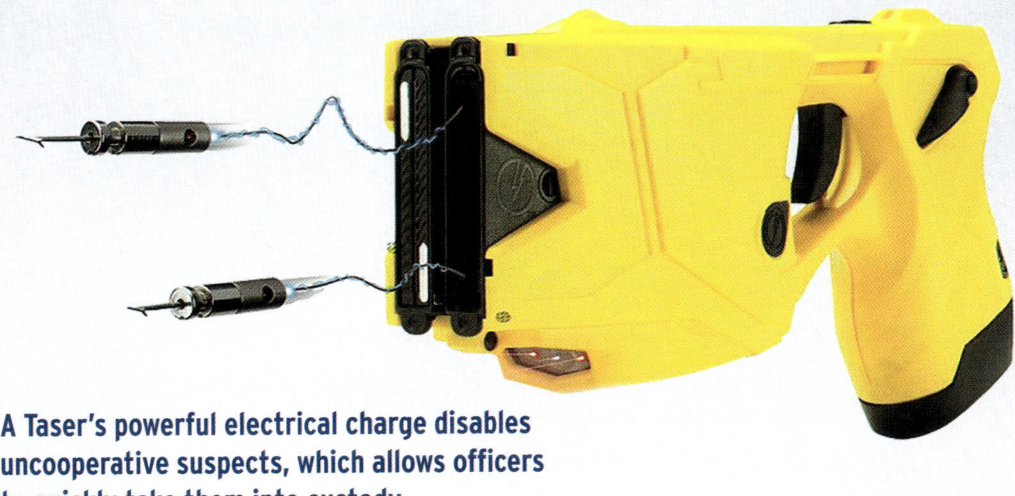

Pepper spray (sometimes called Mace) is another common less-lethal weapon. Most use concentrated capsaicin. It is a natural substance made from the same plant family as chili peppers. When sprayed on the face, it causes temporary burning pain, coughing, and blindness.

Other less-lethal weapons include large rubber bullets or beanbags. They are fired from shotguns or tear-gas launchers. When they strike suspects, it hurts enough to temporarily disable them.

Chapter 8

SQUAD VEHICLES

Cops patrol their assigned neighborhoods on foot, by bike, motorcycle, boat, or even on horseback. However, the most common way is by patrol vehicle (also called a squad car). It is the most important tool officers use every day. It gets them where they are needed quickly. It also holds equipment, including computers and communications gear.

Each agency is responsible for equipping their officers with a fleet of dependable, high performance cars. Common police vehicles today include Ford Explorers, Ford Crown Victorias, Dodge Chargers, and Chevrolet Impalas.

Police packages

Squad vehicles are not that much different from cars purchased by regular civilians. They often have special "police packages," which include sturdier brakes, tires, and suspensions. Engines are not usually modified. Strengthened, tubular push bumpers (push bars) are fitted on some vehicles. They allow squad cars to push disabled vehicles out of the road or to intentionally collide with suspect vehicles.

Squad cars hold all the equipment that patrol officers might need in emergencies.

The interior of a typical Dodge Charger squad car used by the Eden Prairie Police Department in Minnesota.

Most patrol vehicles have a light bar mounted on the roof. It flashes bright red, blue, and white lights that spin and pulse when officers respond to emergencies. Loud sirens also alert people that a police car is on the way.

Patrol cars are equipped with radar. They are either handheld devices or mounted on the squad car. They use radio waves to detect speeding motorists. Some squad cars are equipped with LiDAR units. (LiDAR stands for "light detection and ranging.") They measure speed by using lasers. LiDAR units are very accurate when targeting groups of speeding vehicles.

The back seats of patrol vehicles are where arrested suspects are transported to county jails. The seats are made of hard plastic. That makes them easier to clean if suspects vomit or urinate inside the squad car. Rear doors cannot be opened from the inside. A steel mesh or plastic screen divides the front and back seats, protecting patrol officers.

POLICE 10-CODES

When talking on two-way radios, either to other officers or to police dispatchers, patrol cops often use "10-codes." These are abbreviations for common phrases. They start with the number 10, followed by another number. They keep radio messages brief and understandable. Not every department uses the same 10-codes, but many are similar. Common 10-codes include:

Code	Meaning	Code	Meaning
10-1	Weak signal	10-9	Repeat message
10-2	Good signal	10-10	Fight
10-4	Okay	10-15	Prisoner in custody
10-6	Busy	10-19	Return to station
10-7	Out of service	10-23	Arrived at scene
10-8	In service	10-33	Emergency

Chapter 9

TYPES OF CRIMES

A patrol cop's main duty is to detain or arrest people committing crimes. The crimes can be minor, such as littering. Or they can be very serious, such as murder. Punishment can range from a verbal warning to a trip to the county jail.

Infractions

Infractions are the least serious kind of crime. They are usually punishable by a warning or fine. Examples include minor traffic tickets, littering, or disturbing the peace.

Misdemeanors

Misdemeanors are more serious than infractions. Punishment can include fines and time in jail, usually less than one year. Examples include vandalism and disorderly conduct.

Felonies

Felonies are the most serious kinds of crime. Committing a felony usually results in at least one year in prison. The most serious felonies, such as murder, may result in life imprisonment or the death penalty in some states.

CRIME SCENE DO
SCENE
ON CRIME
NOT ENTE

Chapter 10

TRAFFIC STOPS

Traffic stops occur when patrol cops pull over people suspected of breaking the law. The most common offenses include speeding, running stop signs, being under the influence of drugs or alcohol, aggressive driving, and equipment violations such as broken headlights.

Traffic stops are one of the most dangerous duties a cop can perform. They never know what could happen. It could be an innocent encounter, or it could lead to arrests for outstanding warrants. At worst, a traffic stop might result in violence or a chase. Cops must approach each stop with caution.

Checking for additional crimes

In addition to keeping everyone safe on the roads, traffic stops are an opportunity for police officers to check for additional offenses, such as arrest warrants, or drivers who are using drugs or alcohol. In many cases, cops uncover crimes that are much more serious than the original reason for the traffic stop.

Chapter 11

VEHICLE PURSUITS

Sometimes suspects flee the scene when they are stopped by patrol cops. This can result in dangerous high-speed pursuits. People flee in their vehicles for all kinds of reasons. Usually, they have committed a more serious crime that they don't want discovered. Most commonly, they have drugs or other illegal items in their cars. They may have a suspended license, or arrest warrants from earlier crimes.

Calling off a pursuit

Vehicle pursuits along busy city streets during daytime are so dangerous that they are sometimes called off. Police supervisors can decide that the car chase is not worth the risk of harming innocent people, especially if the traffic stop was because of a minor charge. Officers are also allowed to call off chases on their own. For example, they might decide it is too dangerous to continue the chase if it happens near a school zone. However, at night, with clear roads, it's game on. This is especially true if the fleeing suspect is wanted for a serious crime like armed robbery or murder.

Most car chases last less than 10 minutes. Suspects either give up and stop, or crash their vehicles. Sometimes they exit their cars and flee on foot. They are almost always caught by police officers, who are in better physical shape and can radio nearby cops for help.

SPIKE STRIPS

One way patrol cops can bring a chase to a halt is by using tools called spike strips. They are strips of material that are rolled across the road in front of fleeing vehicles. When run over, small, aluminum spikes embed in the car's tires and break away. The spikes are hollow, which allows air to escape the tire. It quickly deflates, making the car very difficult to drive.

Irvine, CA, police examine a patrol car after it was used to ram and disable a truck used by a crime suspect.

To bring an end to a chase, police sometimes use the front of their squad car to nudge the rear of a fleeing vehicle. This is called a pit maneuver. It usually leads to the suspect losing control of the vehicle and spinning out. That causes it to stall or come to a stop facing the wrong way, giving officers time to box it in with their squad cars. With no escape possible, most suspects give up and are arrested.

Chapter 12

THE STRESSES OF THE JOB

Being a patrol officer is one of the most difficult and stressful jobs a person can have. Every day, cops deal with people at their worst. They encounter drug abusers, alcoholics, and people who beat their spouses or children. They have to arrest hardened criminals, including street gangs, thieves, and murderers. Oftentimes, they must use physical force to place suspects into custody.

On top of the day-to-day difficulties, cops also deal with work-related stress. That can include superiors who are unsupportive, too much paperwork and overtime, and too many overnight shifts. In addition, many cops struggle with family or relationship trouble, or financial difficulties.

Post Traumatic Stress Disorder

Police deal with stress in many ways. Most remain mentally healthy, but all are affected in some way. Some cops become cynical, or emotionally detached from everyday life. Cops who experience severe trauma on the job might develop post-traumatic stress disorder (PTSD). It can lead to depression,

On-the-job stress can sometimes lead to depression, anxiety, and even suicide.

severe anxiety, and suicide. Studies show that up to a third of cops suffer from some form of PTSD sometime during their career. Today, many police departments recognize the need to keep their officers mentally healthy. They have developed programs to recognize PTSD and help officers cope with their stresses.

Despite the hardships, competition for police jobs remains high. Law enforcement is a unique way to serve the community. There are many fulfilling moments, especially helping those in need.

GLOSSARY

arrest – When a person suspected of committing a crime is taken into custody by a law enforcement officer.

BOLO – A term that stands for "be on the lookout." A BOLO alert tell officers a person should be arrested for committing a crime or be brought in for questioning.

detain – When a police officer stops a person for brief questioning, possibly before a formal arrest.

disorderly conduct – Behaving disruptively in public, such as being drunk and talking loudly, or being combative.

dispatch – A communications center for police, firefighters, and other emergency personnel.

epaulets – An ornamental cloth sleeve worn on the shoulder of a uniform.

polygraph – Also called a lie detector test, a machine that measures blood pressure, heart rate, respiration, and electrical conductivity of the skin. An operator is able to tell if a person being questioned is being truthful based on the readings.

radar – A term that stands for "RAdio Detection and RAnging." A device that uses radio waves to detect objects.

semiautomatic – A firearm that shoots once with every pull of the trigger. It automatically reloads, ready for the next shot.

SWAT – A term that stands for "special weapons and tactics." A police unit whose members use special military weapons in dangerous situations, such as riots or hostage rescues.

warrant – An arrest warrant authorizes the police to arrest someone suspected of committing a crime. A search warrant allows the search of a person, vehicle, or building.

ONLINE RESOURCES

To learn more about patrol cops, visit abdobooklinks.com or scan this QR code. These links are routinely monitored and updated to provide the most current information available.

INDEX